500 Affirmations for Manifesting
Love, Romance, and Marriage

Michelle Mann

© **Copyright 2021 - All rights reserved.**

The contents of this book may not be reproduced, duplicated, or transmitted without direct written permission from the author.

Under no circumstances will any legal responsibility or blame be held against the publisher for any reparation, damages, or monetary loss due to the information herein, either directly or indirectly.

Legal Notice:

You cannot amend, distribute, sell, use, quote, or paraphrase any part of the content within this book without the consent of the author.

Disclaimer Notice:

Please note the information contained within this document is for educational and entertainment purposes only. No warranties of any kind are expressed or implied. Readers acknowledge that the author is not engaging in the rendering of legal, financial, medical, or professional advice. Please consult a licensed professional before attempting any techniques outlined in this book.

By reading this document, the reader agrees that under no circumstances is the author responsible for any losses, direct or indirect, which are incurred as a result of the use of the information contained within this document, including, but not limited to, —errors, omissions, or inaccuracies.

Contents

Introduction iii
What Are Love Affirmations? iii
How Do They Work? iv
Positive Affirmations iv

Chapter One
Affirmations and the Law of Attraction 1
What Are the Laws of Attraction? 1
Practicing the Law of Attraction 2
Impact 3
Exercises 4
Pitfalls 5
Seven Steps to Writing Powerful Affirmations 7

Chapter Two
Start with Self-Love 11

Chapter Three
Positive Affirmations for a Healthy, Trusting Relationship 17

Chapter Four
Positive Affirmations to Improve Your Relationship 21

Chapter Five
Positive Affirmations for Love and Marriage — 24

Chapter Six
Positive Affirmations for Marriage Restoration — 30
Affirmations for Her — 32
Affirmations for Him — 33
Affirmations for Appreciating Your Marriage — 34
Affirmations to Fix a Broken Marriage — 35

Chapter Seven
Positive Affirmations to Attract a Specific Person — 36
For a Specific Person — 37
To Attract an Ex — 41

Chapter Eight
Positive Affirmations to Attract Love — 43

Chapter Nine
Ten Elements to Turn Your Affirmations into Results — 49

Conclusion — 52
References — 54

Introduction

Are you trying to attract love to your life? More affection and passion? Or are you looking to strengthen an existing relationship or mend it if it's falling apart? You've picked the right book to do all of that and more.

The Law of attraction is an age-old philosophy that provides you with the solution to what you are looking for. Daily affirmation is an incredibly powerful tool to help you attract what you want, in this case, love, a relationship, and marriage. Using the Law of attraction, affirmations help you channel your emotions the right way, thus directly influencing your life.

What Are Love Affirmations?

Affirmations are positive statements, straightforward and easy to understand, written to reveal your goals. They might sound simple, and yes, at times, they even sound a bit silly, but they have proved themselves to be worthy of trying.

Love affirmations will help you attract what you want in the romantic department. When you repeat affirmations daily, you shape your feelings and thoughts, and that's where the key lies in finding and holding on to loving relationships.

I've provided you with 500 love affirmations to choose from, but I'm also going to show you how to write your own. And, of course, you are free to reword the ones I've provided to suit your needs.

How Do They Work?

There are two primary rules to love:

- To get love, you must give love
- You must love yourself to attract love

These rules mean that to get the love you want, you must be a loving person. The general consensus is that we attract those who are similar to us, or, as the Law of Attraction phrases it – "Like Attracts Like."

Love affirmations can be used to improve current relationships and marriages, your self-love, and attract new love to your life.

Positive Affirmations

When you say positive affirmations daily, you reshape how you feel and think about love and relationships. Keep saying them and your negative thoughts will gradually be replaced with positive ones. Negative thoughts include things like:

- I don't deserve to be loved
- I'm not good enough to be loved
- I'm too old to be in a good, loving relationship
- I will never find real love

These kinds of thoughts are damaging, and constantly thinking and believing them will result in you never finding the love you deserve.

Start using positive affirmations daily, you start a chain reaction, and gradually you will change how you feel and think, leading to a positive change in your life and relationships.

If you are lucky enough to be in a great relationship already, you can also use affirmations to strengthen it further. You can bring more love and happiness and make it last forever.

Let's not waste any more time – read this guide and find the affirmations that fit your needs

Chapter One

Affirmations and the Law of Attraction

Most people have heard of the Law of Attraction, which suggests that we can attract positive results when we think positive thoughts and negative thoughts attract negative outcomes. The Law is based on the firm belief that thoughts are an energy form. Positive energy can bring success in all life areas, including relationships, love, finances, and health.

Over the years, many books have been released on the Law of Attraction, resulting in much attention. However, there is little scientific evidence to prove its claims right now, but that doesn't stop people from believing in it and using it to attract positivity into their lives.

What Are the Laws of Attraction?

Advocates of the Law say there are three universal principles to the Law of Attraction:

1. ***Like Attracts Like*** – suggesting that things attract similar things. In terms of love and relationships, it means that we attract people who are similar to us,

and our thoughts attract similar people too. When you are filled with negative thoughts, it is believed you attract negativity, and positive thoughts attract positivity.

2. *Nature Abhors a Vacuum* – removing negativity from your life leaves a space that can be filled with positivity. This is based on the belief that you can never have a space in your mind or life that is completely empty and, because that space will be filled, you must fill it with positivity.

3. *The Present is Always Perfect* – this is focused on the belief that you can always improve the present moment somehow. You may always think the present is flawed in some way, but this Law says that your energy should be focused on making the present moment perfect for you rather than feeling unhappiness or dread.

Practicing the Law of Attraction

This Law says that you are responsible for creating your own reality – your focus dictates what gets drawn to you and your life. In short, it says that if you believe in something hard enough, it will happen.

You can bring the Law of Attraction into your life in these ways:

- [ ] Be grateful for everything
- [ ] Try to visualize your goals
- [ ] Always look for the positive side of any situation
- [ ] Learn how to recognize negative thinking and banish it

- ☐ Say positive affirmations daily
- ☐ Try seeing a negative event in a more positive light

The Law of Attraction does not claim to be the immediate solution you need to face your challenges, but it can certainly help you to be more optimistic in your outlook. It can also help you keep your motivation levels up to achieve your goals.

Impact

While there is no scientific evidence backing up the Law of Attractions, proponents say it can help you introduce positivity into your life. Some of the main reasons people can benefit from it are:

Spiritual Effects

The reason why some people reap results is that the Law of Attraction taps into their spirituality. That spirituality is already connected to several health benefits, including better overall health, lower stress levels, and less risk of depression.

Some believe the way this works is that the universe or God are aligned with your wishes. This suggests that human beings comprise entirely of energy operating at different frequencies. The only way to change that frequency is to think positive thoughts, particularly being grateful for what you have.

When you use positive and grateful thoughts, you can change that energy's frequency by focusing on what you want instead of being frustrated, thus bringing positivity to your life. How and where you focus your attention will determine what gets attracted, but you must believe that what you are focusing on is already yours or will be soon.

Better Overall Well-Being

By using the Law of Attraction, you can also impact your mental health positively too. When you focus your attention on a new reality, something you want, and with the belief that it will happen, you will take more risks than normal. You will see opportunities you never noticed before, and you open yourself up to more possibilities. By the same token, if you don't believe some can happen, you will miss many opportunities.

If you constantly tell yourself that you don't deserve anything good, your behavior will sabotage any chance of happiness. When you change your feelings and self-talk, you reverse negativity and bring in more positivity, creating healthy, productive patterns. By focusing on the positive, you can shift your life back into an upward ascent rather than spiraling down into permanent negativity.

Optimists are typically happier, healthier, and more successful than pessimists. They can focus on success, pushing their failures to the back.

Many therapy types are based on changing how we talk to ourselves to change our life direction. CBT (cognitive-behavioral therapy) is one of the most used forms of therapy for many different conditions. It is based on identifying negative thoughts and changing them for positive ones, thus leading to better mental health.

Exercises

You can use any or all of the following exercises to use the Law of Attraction in your life:

- *Keep a Journal* – Write your thoughts down to help you identify habitual thought patterns. This will tell if you are an optimist or a pessimist – if the latter, you can learn how to change your negative thoughts for positive ones.

- *Mood Boards* – Mood boards are visual reminders to help you stay positive in your mindset, retain your motivation and focus on achieving your goals.

- *Practice Acceptance* – Rather than focusing your thoughts on all that needs improving in the present, accept it as it is. This doesn't stop you from working towards a positive future, but it does mean you won't keep wishing things were different.

- *Positive Self-talk* – If you are continually critical of yourself, set yourself a goal – each day, you will practice positive self-talk. Although this may be hard to start with, in time, it will become much easier to do and much harder to think negatively and be self-critical.

Pitfalls

All of the books written about the Law of Attraction seem to lead to the same problem – they all suggest that if we believe in good things, they will come to us. That's it, that's all you have to do.

Sadly, these books are misleading because you do need to do more than just believe. An optimistic outlook drives the proactive behaviors that lead to great results. An optimist doesn't succeed purely because of their attitude – it's their behavior that brings about the changes.

By all means, have your beliefs, but if you want them to affect how you behave, you also need other things in your life, including:

- ☐ Challenges
- ☐ Commitment
- ☐ Goals
- ☐ Mindfulness
- ☐ Motivation
- ☐ Support
- ☐ Timelines

Some critics of the Law and the books about it say it could lead people to blame themselves whenever something negative happens, things outside their control, like a major illness, being laid off from work, accidents, etc.

We cannot have full control over everything, but we do control how we respond to things. The Law of Attraction can give you the proactive attitude and optimism needed to face difficult challenges, but it must never be used as a self-blame tool.

How you respond to a challenge dictates your strength. In that way, the Law is useful in encouraging that strength. It must never be applied negatively, though; otherwise, it will not help and be far more destructive.

Now you know what the Law of Attraction is, you can see how it works with daily positive affirmations. Before we look at affirmations for different romantic scenarios, let's see how you can write your own affirmations.

Seven Steps to Writing Powerful Affirmations

While I have provided you with plenty of affirmations in the rest of this book, you should know how to write your own.

Step One – Fill Your Affirmation with Desire

Affirmations don't have to be written down. You can also just speak them from memory. No matter how you do it, make sure you represent the following two elements:

- The words you are saying
- The emotions you are feeling

The first indicates your desired outcome, while the second expresses how you feel about that outcome.

Your words or thoughts tell the universe what you want, and your feelings act as the magnet that attracts them.

Step Two – Always Write in the Present Tense

Your affirmations must state your desire as if it is already achieved. Use terms like "I am," "I am becoming," or "I have."

Instead of saying "I will be healthy," say "I am healthy." Instead of saying, "My relationship will be healthy," say, "I love my partner more than anything else."

If you use the word "will," you are affirming it as something you don't have already, "I am" or "I have" are much more powerful.

Step Three – Speak Your Positive Statement

"I am not shy about public speaking."

There is something wrong with that statement – the word "not."

According to scientists, the human subconscious cannot recognize that word, so the brain interprets that statement as "I am shy about public speaking."

That, right there, tells you the importance of getting your words right. When you write or speak your affirmation, imagine that you have already achieved what you want. The feeling of bliss that comes from this should be what you feel when you say your affirmation.

That example above would be better said as "I am calm when I speak in public."

Because this is such a positive outlook, it leads to the self-belief that can help you overcome negativity and push negative thoughts aside.

Step Four – Repeat Your Affirmations until They Feel True

Affirmations are designed to change your beliefs and thought processes from negative ones to positive ones. For example, let's say you were the victim of an office bully who kept telling you that you were useless at your job. Even though you know it isn't true, you choose to believe it, and this belief gradually worms its way into your subconscious. Slowly, oh so slowly, it became something you truly believed.

Let's reverse that.

Think about the power of believing positive things about yourself.

If you were to tell yourself, every day for months

"I am good at my job."

Eventually, that would be what you believe is the truth. Not that you want to be good at your job, but that you already are.

When you keep telling yourself positive things, making sure your attitude is positive and fearless, you can make positive changes to yourself and your life.

Step Five – Keep It Simple

One of the most effective affirmations is one you can easily remember, no matter where you are or what situation you are in. The shorter they are, the better.

Do not write long affirmations that you will never remember – keep them short and simple.

Something like this

"I am grateful for my life."

Step Six – Your Affirmations Are about You

Affirmations are designed to change you, not someone else.

Don't say, "My best friend knows me better than anyone." That's making it about them, not you. Instead, say, "I know what to do to help my best friend know me better than anyone."

You cannot change someone else, nor can you expect them to. The only change you should want to see is to yourself.

Step Seven – Speak Your Affirmations Every Day

If you continue to say your affirmations every day with a positive mindset, they will feel true to you.

That feeling is a critical part – if you don't include emotion in your affirmations, you are doing nothing more than mechanically reciting a few words.

Write your affirmation and recite it at least three times every day. You can do it whenever you want – morning, lunchtime, evening, whenever feels right.

Put a reminder on your phone or write your affirmation on a sticky note and put it where you will see it.

The idea of reciting your affirmations daily is to rewire your subconscious for success. It will take time, and you must be patient. After all, you can't wash away years of negativity in just a few days.

Chapter Two

Start with Self-Love

The best kind of love is self-love. Not only does loving yourself allow you more gains, but it also helps you attract more from others, enriching your life even further. Love is a magnetic vibration, and when your energy changes, you attract those who share the same or similar energy.

One way you can learn to love yourself is to use self-love affirmations, the simplest and easiest method you can use every day. And you should use them daily, repeated a few times per day, to bring you more confidence, happiness, joy, and self-esteem. You will come to know that you are worthy of being loved. You will get rid of those negative thoughts about yourself. You will welcome positive thoughts and compassion, deepening and strengthening your relationships, not just with others, but with yourself too.

__Here are 100 self-love affirmations for you to choose from – pick the ones that suit you and repeat them several times a day, every day.__

I love my body and everything it does for me

I am enough

I respect my boundaries

I am worthy of being loved

I choose myself today

I love who I am

I am loved

I deserve love

I am always kind to myself

Love flows out of me

I am beautiful from the inside out

I love my individuality

I deserve to be happy

I push negative self-talk away

I am whole

I have everything I need within me

I control my happiness

I will achieve my goals

I unconditionally accept myself for who I am

I don't allow fears to control me

I am grateful for everything I have

I always make time to look after myself

I love me, and accept me

It is easy and natural for me to love myself

I am resilient and strong

I am successful

I have an infinite capacity for love

I release those who don't respect me

I leave the past behind and live only in the present

Every day, I grow a little more

I forgive myself for my mistakes and learn from them

I am a true work of art

I am valued

I feel deeply

I am open and ready for love

I love my body

I can achieve whatever I want to

I overcome challenges easily and gracefully

I have a warm, loving heart

I am who I need to be right now

I send love to my doubts and fears

I brush negativity aside

I have a deep belief in myself

I will say no to anything not in my best interests

I push aside anything that doesn't serve me

I accept all compliments gratefully and easily

I release the need for suffering

I have much to offer

I love everything about me that makes me who I am

I am cloaked in loving energy from the universe

My life is joyful and loving

I always have and will continue to do my best in everything

I have achieved many good things

I respect myself

My life is balanced and harmonious

The power is with me to change my world

I choose not to apologize for who I am

I am not my flaws or my mistakes

Other people accept me for who I am and love me for it

I put myself and my needs first

I am filed with confidence

My mind is overflowing with loving thoughts

I attract loving, positive people to me

The more practice I put in to love myself, the more loveable I am

I allow love into my life

I love myself more each day

Love flows from inside of me freely

If I don't succeed, I practice self-compassion

I honor my path in life

I honor my limitations and respect them

I have much to love about me and who I am

My life reflects my inner love

I only need my own approval

I shine with love

I love being with me

I don't need anyone to know that I am worthy

I attract light and love

I do not need to judge myself negatively

From today, I choose to love myself more

I can love completely and fully

My body is a temple that I care for and love

I am powerful and full of confidence

I trust that I can get through the tough times

My intuition is solid

My life is filled with opportunities for happiness, success, and love

I reward myself for being dedicated and working hard

I am balanced

The universe always supports me

I have a deep love for my body

I can love myself whenever I want to

Loving me means I can love others

I have a positive, healing effect on those around me

My life is worthy of celebration

I am proud of who I am

I choose positivity in my life

My body is the best friend I have

I choose to look after my body and health

I am my life's healer

I choose love

I can be loved

Chapter Three

Positive Affirmations for a Healthy, Trusting Relationship

It doesn't matter how strong and intense your love is initially; the honeymoon phase will begin to wear off. However, you can transform that excess energy into something deeper – more love, respect, and appreciation for your partner, bringing in better understanding, fewer arguments, more togetherness, and less separation.

We don't get lessons on relationships, love, ideals, qualities, or communication when we go to school, and that's part of the reason why many of us fail in our first attempts at love. However, there are many ways a loving and trusting relationship can be sustained, and by far, the easiest way is to use daily affirmations. When you repeat these every day, you learn to take responsibility for your feelings, thoughts, and actions, not to mention setting the intention to have a healthy and trusting relationship.

Love doesn't come with conditions – it is we who place those conditions on experiencing love, and it is we who pay the price.

Here are fifty affirmations – choose the right ones to help you maintain a good loving relationship with your partner.

I am secure, loved, and cherished in my relationship

I can freely be myself in my relationship

I deeply appreciate and respect my partner

I am comfortable in telling my partner how I feel and what I need

My partner and I easily communicate with one another

I am cherished and loved for who I am

I can see things from my partner's point of view

I am free to set my boundaries in my relationship

My partner and I do everything we can to support one another

I have a healthy relationship with my partner

I build up the strength of my love for my partner

When I am with my partner, I am always true to myself

I can communicate my needs to my partner effectively

I deeply respect my partner

I can draw boundaries when I have to

I love my partner unconditionally

I take time to think of ways to help my partner succeed

I take time to consider my partner's needs

I can make time and space for myself when I need to

I always consider my partner's perspective

My partner and I draw closer every day

I will improve my relationship every day

I will care for and respect my partner every day

I will always talk to my partner

I continually deepen my relationship with my partner

I will tell my partner what I need

I will be the best partner

I will always be honest about our relationship

I will continue to work on maintaining a healthy and trusting relationship

I feel our love growing deeper by the day

I will always communicate respectfully with my partner

I feel cherished and loved by my partner

All my efforts in building a loving, trusting relationship are worth it

A normal day for me includes a loving, trusting relationship

I will do everything in my power to maintain a healthy relationship

My partner's feelings are important to me

It is important to me to have healthy, happy relationships

It is easy for me to draw the right boundaries

I deserve a happy, healthy, trusting relationship

I am good at communicating honestly and openly

I love, respect, and trust my partner

My partner loves, respects, and trusts me

My trust in my partner strengthens each day

I am comfortable in my trust in my partner

There is complete trust between us

I am confident in my partner's choices

I believe in my partner's integrity

My partner and I have complete trust between us

I have confidence in my partner

I feel blessed to have a partner I trust deeply and unconditionally.

Chapter Four

Positive Affirmations to Improve Your Relationship

When you are finding your relationship tough, it isn't always easy to know what to do. Each situation and each person is different, which can make it hard to know which way to go. Conversely, some things are easy and helpful, regardless of the situation, and daily affirmations are one of those things.

Affirmations have been in existence for centuries in secular and religious contexts. There is also some scientific evidence supporting their power in bringing about positive changes to your life.

They are simple, free and you can use them anywhere, at any time you want. You might think it strange that affirmations can help you improve your relationship, but perspective and attitude play large roles in your interaction with your partner. Daily affirmations help you see what your partner is doing right because that is where your focus is.

Please, don't think these affirmations are the only solution to fixing what's wrong with your relationship. They are designed to help you see the best in your partner and change your state of mind, so you are present in the relationship.

To that end, I've provided 31 affirmations for you to choose from.

I am in a loving relationship that will last

My partner and I find it easy to communicate

My partner and I solve our problems respectfully and peacefully

I give love freely in my relationship, and I receive it too

I love my partner and accept them for who they are, no matter what

I am comfortable being myself

I give my relationship all the attention and care it needs

I feel free enough to reveal who I am to my partner

My partner and I have healthy boundaries

My partner and I love each other strongly and powerfully

My partner and I deserve love and deserve to love

My partner and I deserve a happy, long-lasting, trusting relationship

My partner and I are committed to a loving, strong partnership

My love grows stronger for my partner every day

My partner and I are accepting of our respective weaknesses

and strengths

My partner and I give all the attention, time, and care our relationship needs

My partner and I love spending quality time together

I support my partner, and my partner supports me

My partner and I feel safe and comfortable together

I love to spend quality, intimate time with my partner

The love between my partner and me is strong enough to weather the fights

I and content and happy in my relationship

I am grateful for everything my partner does for me

My partner knows my flaws, accepts them, and helps me become better

My partner and I are comfortable talking about thoughts and problems

My partner respects my privacy, and I respect theirs

I am myself whenever I am with my partner

My partner and I make time to talk every day

My partner ensures I am cherished, loved, and secure all the time

I am confident in the trust my partner, and I have for one another

Our relationship is filled with love, respect, and trust.

Chapter Five

Positive Affirmations for Love and Marriage

Marriage affirmations don't just help when you are getting married. They can also help preserve your marriage for life, provided you repeat them daily, with a positive, faithful attitude, allowing no distractions to take your focus away.

When you repeat affirmations daily, you focus your thoughts on your marriage, partner, and love, excluding all else, and what you focus on will grow.

If you are worried about not being married, you need to look at what is going on in your mind. Distractions are the biggest reason why people remain unmarried. A lack of attention, being too busy with work or other things leads to more negativity and less chance of attracting a love prospect. Or it may be that you are looking at marriage from entirely the wrong perspective.

In today's modern world, men and women are looking to make a career for themselves, and most other things are pushed to the back seat. Marriages are neglected until it's too later to find the right person to marry or until your marriage falls apart.

We neglect our marriages, our partners because our career

is more important – we eat, breathe and sleep it. We focus on our careers, allowing them to grow and marriages fall behind, withering and dying.

When you say marriage affirmations daily, they help you to get your priorities right. When your primary focus is on marriage, your prospects increase, and you begin to take the right actions to go in the right direction.

If you are already married, you may find that you or your partner are too distracted to focus. It could be your career getting in the way, an affair, ill health, anything that can take your focus away. Again, affirmations can help you to get things back on track.

But saying these affirmations daily must go hand in hand with actively working on your marriage and your mindset to change its direction. You must be actively interested in your partner. You must want to go out for dinner, go on vacation, celebrate birthdays and anniversaries, and do all you can to keep the spark alight.

Choose your affirmations from the 72 listed below and repeat them several times a day – every day!

I love being loved by my spouse

I love being in love

My marriage grows stronger and deeper each day

I love the security and safety my marriage brings

I love the trusting, secure, loving marriage I am in

I enjoy how being loved and cherished makes me feel

My marriage is bliss, and I achieved that

I am very happy and do all I can to make my marriage work, and last

My partner and I have a powerful love for one another, and this protects our marriage

My spouse and I are best friends

My marriage will be strong forever

Romance runs strongly through my marriage, filling it with joy, love, and happiness

I love my marriage being more romantic each day

I love being showered with romance by my spouse

I find romance everywhere, in everything, and everyone

I allow my spouse to delight and surprise me with romance

I love my marriage being filled with romance

I give romance and receive it happily

I can have romance in the present moment

I am open to more romance

Romance loves me, and I love romance

I happily thrive in a supportive, happy, loving marriage

I feel secure with my spouse

I have a loving, warm, and committed marriage

I love loving, and I love to be loved by my spouse

I love that my generous, kind, amazing spouse loves and treasures me

I accept perfect love in the present moment

I live my life knowing I am loved

I attract relationships that are for the highest good

I love having fantastic conversations with my spouse, friends, and family

I love the company of my best friends

I love to have fun and laugh a lot in my marriage

I love knowing that my marriage is harmonized with my highest good

I accept that my spouse loves and treasures me for who I am

I give love freely and completely and receive it in my marriage

I love that my family, friends, and spouse support me

I love sharing the real me with my spouse

I know with all my heart and my being that the universe brings only the most loving, supportive, and awesome relationships

I enjoy what my marriage gives me and all the things that make me happy

I have deep appreciation for my spouse for all they do for me and our marriage

My spouse and I decide to love each other every day

I am making my marriage stronger every day

I choose to listen before reacting out of anger

I accept the chance to be the first to apologize

I am devoted and loyal to my spouse

I support my spouse in whatever they want to do

Together, my spouse and I are strong

Together, we live a life of gratefulness

Every day I take the chance to learn about my spouse

I respect my spouse and the person they are rather than the person I want them to be

I choose to place my focus only on the positive daily

My marriage is built on trust, respect, and love

My spouse and I accept we have differences and don't judge

I have unconditional love for my spouse

My spouse and I communicate openly every day

I provide my spouse with the space they need to be who they are within our marriage

My spouse and I laugh regularly

Our marriage goes from strength to strength

I accept we have bad days, but we carry on together

I must forgive my spouse every day

My spouse cannot resist me, and I will not deny them when possibly

I will regularly ask myself how I can better show my love to my spouse

There is nothing we cannot face and beat together

My spouse and I have honest and open communication

My spouse will always be my best friend

I will control my temper and tongue when angry, and I will fight a fair fight if we disagree on something

I want to kiss my spouse every day

My love for my spouse is passionate

My marriage is truly the perfect match

I accept and respect the differences between my spouse and me

I believe strongly and deeply in my marriage

"I will be patient and kind. I will not envy, or boast, or be proud. I will not dishonor others, or be self-seeking, or easily angered, nor will I keep a record of wrongs. I will not delight in evil, but I will rejoice in the truth. I will always protect, always trust, always hope, always persevere. I know love never fails." (1 Corinthians 13:4-8)

Chapter Six

Positive Affirmations for Marriage Restoration

Enjoying life as a married person requires that you have a healthy and happy marriage, but this isn't always the case. Too many people jump straight to divorce without first trying to see if they can fix the marriage.

It doesn't matter whether you are a newly married couple or you've been married for years. Disagreements and conflicts arise and if you want to try fixing them before they go too far, try daily affirmations.

Daily affirmations can help you get past the obstacles that stand between you and a happy marriage, a marriage you both thought was once so worthwhile. Unhappiness can change, even ruin a marriage and your life, and it's important to get back to what you had.

Here are 73 affirmations for you to choose from to help build your relationship and restore your marriage to its former glory:

I am completely committed to my marriage

I understand my spouse and appreciate them for all they do to keep our marriage strong

My spouse supports and encourages me to follow my dreams

I accept my spouse for who they are

My marriage is built on a solid foundation of trust, respect, and love

I love my spouse unconditionally

My spouse loves me unconditionally

The love my spouse gives me helps me to become a stronger and better person

My marriage is the best gift from God and the universe

I love falling in love with my spouse every day, enjoying it like it is the first time all over again

My spouse and I are 100% faithful to one another

I love looking forward to spending the rest of my life with my spouse

I choose love

I am grateful for being able to share my life with my spouse

I am truly blessed to have my spouse in my life

I appreciate all my spouse does for me

I welcome all the challenges our marriage brings as ways to learn and make us stronger together

I am committed to my spouse

I am devoted to my spouse

I respect my spouse's individuality

I love listening to all my spouse has to say

I accept my spouse's decisions and embrace all they do

My marriage is my priority

I will never forget why my spouse and I got married

I love my spouse unconditionally and respect them always

I am calm and honest in how I express my vulnerability and emotions to my spouse

My spouse and I are committed to making our marriage stronger each day

My spouse and I face our challenges together with strength and love

I appreciate that my spouse and I have differences and respect them

My spouse and I will never hold grudges and will always work through our problems

My spouse and I make the best team

Affirmations for Her

I communicate constructively and in a healthy way with my husband

I appreciate my husband because he brings out my good side and embraces my strengths

I freely give my husband love without any fears

I always look for ways to love my husband more, so he

doesn't need to question my feelings

I make my expectations and intentions clear in our marriage, so there is no confusion

We have a healthy marriage with no resentment or guilt

My husband loves me

I love my husband with all my heart

I make sure I show appreciation for everything he does for me

I am beautiful, and my husband is deeply attracted to me

I accept my need for attention comes from insecurity and banish it from my life

I constantly look for ways to make our marriage better

I'm fine with my husband having female friends

I am completely secure in myself

I relish the thought of growing old with my husband

I love to do things that make my husband happy.

Affirmations for Him

I am vulnerable and willing to be that way

I am constructive in expressing my feelings and emotions to my wife

I love including my wife in my life

I love making my wife happy

I make sure my wife knows I find her desirable and beautiful, so she knows she is secure with me

I love my wife deeply and tell her that every day

My wife loves me deeply

I enjoy sharing my life and look forward to spending our future together

I love telling my wife all about my day because it brings us together

My wife and I communicate well and easily with each other

I am comfortable talking to my wife about my emotions

I am comfortable in letting my wife see my vulnerable side because she does not judge me

I love how my wife makes me feel strong and manly

I give my wife love freely and with no fear

I feel my wife appreciates me for my efforts, and it helps me be better and stronger

I support my wife in the decisions she makes, but I am comfortable in calmly addressing her when I feel she is wrong

I love doing things to show my wife I love her

Affirmations for Appreciating Your Marriage

I appreciate my spouse with all my being

I am grateful to have my spouse in my life

I consider my marriage as sacred

I am blessed to share my life with my spouse

Affirmations to Fix a Broken Marriage

My spouse and I will always remember why we love one another

I will love my spouse, no matter what

My spouse and I will work through our problems together

Our love for one enough is strong, and we can get through this together

I choose to focus on all the good in my spouse

Chapter Seven

Positive Affirmations to Attract a Specific Person

Is there a specific person in your life you want to attract? Have you thought about using positive daily affirmations to help you? If not, you should.

It doesn't matter who you are. If you want a love relationship with a certain person, you can have it. That is how positive affirmations work. That is how powerful they are. However, you must be in the right frame of mind for them to work, and you must be prepared to do what it takes to achieve your goal.

Besides communicating with people, you can use your mind to attract someone. Even if your previous relationships have left you with a sour taste or had bad experiences, you can make things work for you. With a positive mind, you can use daily affirmations to eliminate negative thoughts, kick uncertainty into touch and fill your mind with certainty.

Daily affirmations can help you attract the person you want and embark on a healthy relationship, forget your past, and place your focus firmly on the future. However, before you start reciting your daily affirmations, there are a few things you need to do:

1. Be specific about the person you want to attract

At all stages in life, everyone needs someone. You may be looking for a relationship with a new person or want to get back together with an ex. No matter who it is, you must be specific about who it is, in great detail, which means you must be utterly convinced that this is the person you want to spend the rest of your life with.

If you need to, write the person's name on a piece of paper, together with a detailed description. Include any details you think are relevant, including what you like so much about them. This is your goal so be accurate. If you make your goal uncertain or non-specific, you won't get the result you want.

2. Be optimistic

Understand that everything must go through a process so, if you don't see the results you want straight away, don't be disheartened and don't give up. Positive affirmations will only work once all shreds of doubt are removed from your mind, which can take time. So, don't expect your chosen love interest to knock on your day the day after you say your first positive affirmations. That kind of expectation is a recipe for disaster because it will only bring disappointment.

Are you ready?

Here are 79 affirmations to choose from, starting with those you use to attract a new person to you:

For a Specific Person

Don't forget to replace "specific person" with the name of the person you want to attract:

I will be eternally grateful to have (specific person) in my life

(Specific person) and I would be a great match

I am arrestable to (specific person)

My relationship with (specific person) will be joyous

I will feel cherished, loved, and fulfilled in a relationship with (specific person)

I sense a divine love connects me with (specific person)

I am in heaven when I think of a relationship with (specific person)

(Specific person) will be the most loving person in my life, and I will enjoy every minute of it

I will deeply enjoy a relationship with (specific person)

(specific person) will love me deeply

I will be (specific person's) first priority, the most important thing in their life

(Specific person) will always think about me

(Specific person) is deeply attracted to me

(Specific person) only has eyes for me

(Specific person) is attracted only to me

Me and (specific person) will have a fulfilling relationship

(specific person) will always be attracted to me

My relationship with (specific person) will be deeply fulfilling

My relationship with (specific person) will be healthy and trusting

(Specific person) will always find comfort with me

(Specific person) thinks highly of me and our relationship

(Specific person) cares about me and my feelings

(Specific person) is very affectionate towards me

(Specific person) treats me with the highest level of respect

(Specific person) is obsessed with me and making me happy

(Specific person) feels they are lucky to have me

(Specific person) and I share a happy relationship

(Specific person) and I appreciate each other and respect each other and ourselves

(Specific person) cherishes and adores me

(Specific person) is desperate to spend the rest of their life together with me

I am comfortable and able to be myself around (specific person)

(Specific person) is thankful I am in their life

(specific person) encourages me and supports me in everything I do

The love between me and (specific person) grows stronger every day

(Specific person) always sees the best in me

(Specific person) considered meeting me as the best thing to happen to them

(Specific person) feels that I understand them in ways no one else does

My relationship with (specific person) is loving and harmonious

(Specific person) loves me unconditionally

The bond between me and (specific person) grows stronger as each day passes

(Specific person) and I share something very special

(Specific person) always wants to make me happy

(Specific person) loves and cherishes me for who I am

I love myself and am prepared and ready to love (specific person)

I am ready to receive love from (specific person)

I trust that God will connect me with (specific person)

I will give love in abundance and receive it from (specific person)

I am ready to have a healthy relationship with (specific person)

I want nothing more than to spend my life with (specific person)

I accept love, I give love, and I spread love to all around me

I am happy and ready to spend time with (specific person)

I deserve to be loved by (specific person)

My true love will love me and give me the attention I need and deserve

My soul and their soul are ready for a deep connection

I have learned self-love and will use it to love (specific person) completely and make them feel worthy

I am worthy of love, of receiving attention

Love is waiting for me with (specific person), and I am ready for it

I will find the right person for me

I will find (specific person) and spend the rest of my life with them

To Attract an Ex

If you want to rekindle a friendship and relationship with someone you were with previously, you can also use positive daily affirmations to attract them back to you:

I know that (specific person) is my soulmate

I will be totally faithful to (specific person)

I accept (specific person) for who they are

I want (specific person) to be back in my life

I want to get together with (specific person) again

(Specific person) and I were meant to be

I am ready to be the person (specific person) wants me to be

I love (specific person) deeply, and I want to spend the rest of my life with them

(Specific person) and I are a perfect match

(Specific person) and I improve each other's lives

I will give (specific person) more than enough love

I will willingly receive love from (specific person)

I want to grow old with (specific person)

I want to fall in love with (specific person) every day

I will work hard to make (specific person) happy

I will always put (specific person's) feelings first

(Specific person) will put my feelings first

(Specific person) will do everything to make me happy

We will be comfortable and ready to rekindle our relationship

We are meant to be together.

Chapter Eight

Positive Affirmations to Attract Love

We all desire love in our lives, be it from ourselves or others. By saying daily love affirmations, you can help attract that love to you in great amounts.

Some people feel unworthy of love and loathe themselves. If you cannot or do not cultivate self-love, you don't stand a chance of attracting love to you from anyone else. Daily affirmations can help put loving thoughts back into your mind, help you be more confident that someone can give you the love you desire and deserve.

Many people ask if love affirmations work. They do work, but only if you accompany them with the right mindset and follow them with actions that reflect your mindset. For example, if you choose to say "I am worthy of being loved" as one of your daily affirmations, you must act as though you are worthy by being good to yourself.

You must also be out there to attract love. It's no good saying affirmations to attract it if you stay shut in your house. Thoughts and feelings play such a large role in the way we act and, while you cannot always control your feelings, your thoughts can influence and affect your feelings - when you focus on finding love, you focus on doing the things that make it possible to happen.

With all of that said, here are some affirmations that will help you attract more romantic love into your life.

Here are the last 95 affirmations you will need, aimed at helping you attract love:

I deserve affection and to be loved

I love myself and are fully open to being loved

I love to give love and receive it

The more love I give, the more I receive it

The universe will help you find your true love

My life is full of love

I am surrounded by love wherever I go

I am grateful for the affection and love I get

I am ready for love

I am worthy of being loved

I have opened my heart to receive love

My partner will always love me, despite my flaws

I push down my barriers to receiving love

I will be loved and accepted for who I am

I am worthy of being part of a romantic love story

My actions will attract a trusting and respectful relationship

I will reflect everything I desire in a partner

I will be happy with my relationship

My relationship will be full of love and affection

I am ready and willing to allow new love into my life

I choose self-love, and my partner will also love me

My next partner will be worthy of marriage

I embody what I want to receive from others

Love is a big part of my life

I give and receive love equally

My heart is big enough to care for the people I love

I attract who I want in my life

My partner will give me love whenever I want it

I can connect strongly with another person

My heart is no longer broken

Love will flow into my life

I find it easy to develop natural connections with people

My life is love itself

I am grateful to the person who will love me

I am the person my next partner will love

I will have an honest, open relationship

I am like a magnet, attracting love to me

Every day, I will love my partner more

Every day, my partner will love me more

My relationship will be passionate

I am surrounded only by loving people

My love life will be the best

Love is perfectly possible for me

My next partner will be the best I have ever known

My next relationship will last for the rest of my life

I will find my true love

My true love will find me

I will be appreciated and loved for who I am

The right person for me is out there

I attract love and healthy relationships

I receive abundant love

My mind is open to finding love where I don't expect to

I'm grateful that I can love and accept myself

I freely give my heart, opening it to the heart of my one true love

I am loved more than I thought I could be

I am open to receiving truly amazing love

I have room in my life for a wonderful, loving partner

The universe will provide my soulmate for me

My partner will show me the deepest, most passionate love

My next partner and I will trust and love each other for life

I will be in a relationship where I am treated right

I will treat my next partner right, with the respect and kindness they deserve

I deserve to be loved and receive affection

I will attract the right kind of person for me

I love me, and my partner will love me too

I am worthy of a loving relationship

I deserve true happiness in my life

I am overflowing with love

I love who I am

I am open to being loved

Love surrounds me

My next relationship will be healthy

I will allow the universe to lead me to my true love

I deserve for my next relationship to be passionate

The universe will provide passion and romance for me

I will only attract the most trusting and healthiest of relationships

I happily give and receive love every day

Everywhere I go, I find love

I will be in a relationship with a person who respects me

I will be in a relationship with someone I trust implicitly

I am open to being in a loving relationship with the right

person

Love begins with me

I am love, and I am light

Love comes naturally to me

I am a charismatic person

I can be loved

The more love I show a person, the more they will show me

I am always in fulfilling relationships

I am grateful for all the love in my life

I find it easy to share love

I attract real connections

My heart is open to love

I find it easy to connect with others

The universe wants me to have the most wonderful, fulfilling love

I am love

Chapter Nine

Ten Elements to Turn Your Affirmations into Results

If you want your affirmations to reap the right results, you must ensure these ten elements are included:

1. Know What You Want in life

Know exactly what you want to change, in this case, attract love, fix your relationship or marriage or even learn to love yourself better. List what is already going well and where you want to see changes. From that list, choose one area to start with – the rest can come later.

2. Be SMART

Every goal you make should be SMART:

- ☐ Specific
- ☐ Measurable
- ☐ Achievable/Actionable (your choice)
- ☐ Realistic
- ☐ Timely

If you can't meet all these in one go, do make sure that your goals are as focused as they can be. That way, you can create the right image in your mind when you speak your affirmations.

3. Keep Your Focus on the Positives

If you want true success, your affirmations must be stated positively – never speak in negative tense. The human brain doesn't focus on whole sentences, only on specific words. If you say, "I do not want to be alone," your brain will hear, "I want to be alone." It focuses on "alone" and cannot recognize the word "not." You should rephrase it as "I want to be with someone."

4. Keep Your Focus on the Present

Your affirmations should be written and spoken in the present tense, not in the past or future, where you can. If you can write your statements like this, your subconscious will believe it is happening. Where you can't do this, use future tense – never use past tense.

5. Your Affirmations Should Be in the First-Person

Don't use "you" when you speak your affirmations – use "I." For example, say "I am happy" and not "you are happy." This will give your brain a better sense of identity. If needs be, add your own name to the affirmation.

6. Connect Your Feelings to Your Behavior

When you tie behavior to feelings, they reflect in your actions. Positive feelings result in positive actions because pleasure is the reward you will want over and again. Use words that strengthen your affirmations and make sure your actions match your feelings.

7. *Visualize a Detailed Image*

Use the previous steps to visualize your affirmation and keep it in your mind while you say your words. Be very specific on where and who you are and how you feel. Don't forget – feelings are great motivators.

8. *Practice Daily*

Don't say your affirmations once a week and expect them to work. You must practice if you want to turn negative thoughts into positive ones, so be prepared to say them several times a day, every day. Eventually, your behaviors, thoughts, and feelings will turn into positive ones.

9. *Be Aware of Triggers*

You may not be ready to hear some affirmations. For example, kind words can hurt some people, especially if they have been victims of abuse, and it can unlock some powerful, bad memories. If this is the case for you, it could be that your affirmations take longer to take effect – stick with it because it will work. Take your time and be nice to yourself.

10. Practice the Best Way For You

There isn't a set way to practice daily positive affirmations. Create your own space and your own way of practicing. You can use the affirmations in this book or create your own; it's entirely up to you.

The real key to success is consistent practice with the right mindset. Visualize your affirmations in a positive light, keep your thoughts positive and keep going.

Conclusion

The one question that gets asked frequently is, do these positive love affirmations really work? The answer is yes and no. First, here's why they may not work.

If you are repeating your chosen affirmations every day but not getting results, it could be that you have chosen the wrong ones. When you say your affirmations, do they make you feel happy? Hopeful? If not, choose some new ones.

I've provided 500, but there are thousands more, and you can write your own. Whichever way you do it, your affirmations must resonate with your feelings and thoughts – you will know if they do. They should light a fire within you, give you an uplifting boost. You can choose what you think are the best affirmations in the world, but if they are not in tune with your emotions, they won't work.

Something else to note is that your affirmations should not be specific. Saying something like "I love being in a relationship with Simon," for example, is far too restrictive, whereas "I love being in a relationship with my husband/partner" is more generic, and it takes a lot of worry and anxiety away.

Affirmations are only one manifestation tool. You can affirm religiously every day, but they won't work if you aren't trying in other areas. One of the most important ways to help your dreams come true is to have a positive outlook. Saying your affirmations with a negative outlook simply cancels them out.

Affirmations have been used for centuries, but it was only when the Law of Attraction came into being that the manifestation paths were drawn up, and affirmations were developed as we know them today. Lots of successful people have used daily affirmations and say that's where their success lies.

Using positive love affirmations can give you the kickstart you need to find the love you deserve. Use them to keep you free of worries, calm, and keep negative thoughts at bay. Used right, they can get you back on track should you stray from the path.

Used right, love affirmations are there to remind you of what you desire in life.

Good luck in your journey to finding true love in your life.

References

"30 Powerful Positive Affirmations to Attract a Specific Person." 2020. PositiveAffirmationsly. November 27, 2020. https://positiveaffirmationsly.com/positive-affirmations-attract-specific-person/.

"34 Positive Marriage Affirmations for Couples to Use Daily." 2013. Our Family Lifestyle. February 28, 2013. https://ourfamilylifestyle.com/marriage-affirmations/.

"40 Affirmations for Love, Romance and Relationships." 2014. Apply the Law of Attraction. March 3, 2014. https://www.applythelawofattraction.com/affirmations-love-romance/.

"70 Love & Relationship Affirmations You Can Start Today." n.d. https://www.abundancenolimits.com/relationship-affirmations/.

"74 Affirmations to Find Love with a Specific Person [That Work]." 2021. ByDeze. June 23, 2021. https://bydeze.com/positive-love-affirmations-for-specific-person/.

"100 Self Love Affirmations to Build Your Self Esteem." 2019. Through the Phases. April 26, 2019. https://www.throughthephases.com/self-love-affirmations/.

antimaximalist. 2021. "45 Love Affirmations to Attract Love into Your Life." Antimaximalist. April 20, 2021. https://

antimaximalist.com/affirmations-for-finding-love/.

Harriet. 2018. "How to Write Powerful Affirmations for the Law of Attraction." Subconscious Servant. September 28, 2018. https://subconsciousservant.com/how-to-write-powerful-affirmations-for-the-law-of-attraction/.

"Marriage & Couples Affirmations to Build a Stronger Relationship." n.d. https://motivationping.com/couples-marriage-affirmations/.

Pangilinan, Jessa. 2021. "35 Relationship Affirmations to Grow Your Love Together." Happier Human. February 25, 2021. https://www.happierhuman.com/relationship-affirmations/.

Perez, Dawn. 2020. "40 Affirmations to Attract Love, Romance and a Healthy Relationship – Wild Simple Joy." Wildsimplejoy.com. January 23, 2020. https://wildsimplejoy.com/affirmations-for-finding-love/.

Scott, Elizabeth. 2007. "Understanding and Using the Law of Attraction in Your Life." Verywell Mind. Verywellmind. February 19, 2007. https://www.verywellmind.com/understanding-and-using-the-law-of-attraction-3144808.

Taylor, Author. 2020. "51 Self-Love Affirmations to Feel & Attract More Love." Taylor's Tracks. August 10, 2020. https://www.taylorstracks.com/self-love-affirmations/.

"The Best Relationship Affirmations to Improve Connections." n.d. Selfpause. https://selfpause.com/affirmations/relationship-affirmations/.

www.ingramcontent.com/pod-product-compliance
Lightning Source LLC
Chambersburg PA
CBHW051710090426
42736CB00013B/2627